# B is for Boat

C is for Car

Our books use a matte finish to reduce glare and create a softer, more comfortable reading

# A to Z

# Not Just ABCs

## Wrtten By T.L.Derby

## Illustrated By Alejandro Echavez

MacLaren-Cochrane Publishing

©2024 T.L. Derby

Cover and Interior Art©2024 Alejandro Echavez

**A to Z, not just ABC Dyslexic Edition**



First Edition

ISBN Softcover: 978-1-64372-325-9

A is for Apple

# D is for Dinosaurs

# E is for Elephants

# F is for Fish

# G is for Gorilla

# H is for Home

I is for Igloo

# J is for Jellybeans

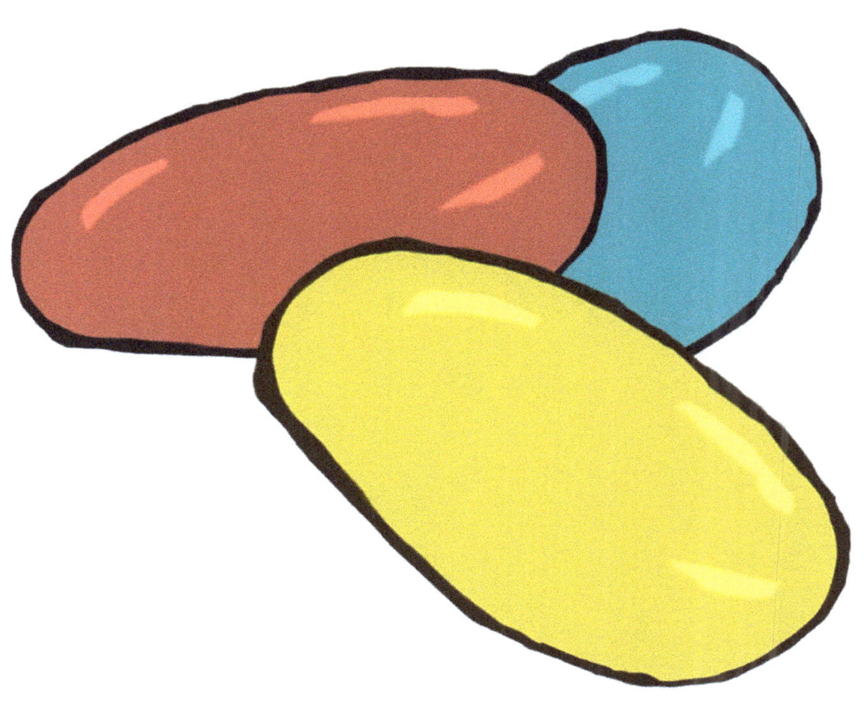

# K is for Kangaroo

# L is for Lion

# M is for Mouse

# N is for Nest

# O is for Octopus

# P is for Plane

Q is for queen

# R is for Raccoon

S is for Seal

# T is for Truck

U is for Umbrella

# V is for Vase

# W is for Walrus

# X is for X-ray

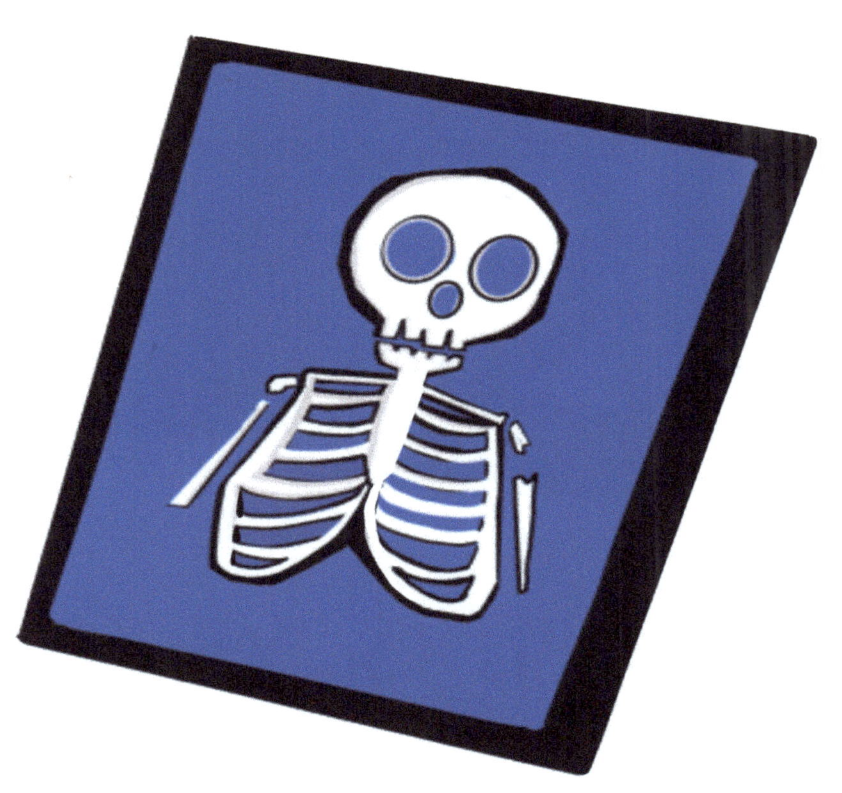

# Y is for Yarn

# Z is for Zebra

A to Z, we've
had so much fun,
Not just A B C,
we've learned each one.

From apples to zebras,
the journey's begun,
Learning is magic,
enjoyed by everyone.

# What is Dyslexie Font?

Each letter is given its own identity making it easier for
people with dyslexia to be more successful at reading.

The Dyslexia font:
1 Makes letters easier to distinguish
2 Offers more ease, regularity and joy in reading
3 Enables you to read with less effort
4 Gives your self-esteem a boost
5 Can be used anywhere, anytime and on (almost) every device
6 Does not require additional software or programs
7 Offers the simplest and most effective reading support

The Dyslexia font is specially designed for people with dyslexia,
in order to make reading easier – and more fun. During the
design process, all basic typography rules and standards were
ignored. Readability and specific characteristics of dyslexia are
used as guidelines for the design.

Designed to make reading clearer and more enjoyable for people with
dyslexia, Dyslexie uses heavy base lines, alternating stick and tail
lengths, larger openings, and semicursive slants to ensure that each
character has a unique and more easily recognizable form.

Our books are not just for children to enjoy, they are also for adults
that have dyslexia that want the experience of reading
to the children in their lives.

Learn more and get the font for your digital devices at
www.dyslexiefont.com

www.ingramcontent.com/pod-product-compliance
Lightning Source LLC
Chambersburg PA
CBHW040904070726
47599CB00038B/2301